60 Years of Princesshay

Peter Thomas

CONSTRUCTION TO DEMOLITON

With Photographs by
PETER THOMAS
&
The Isca Historical Photographic Collection
(Est 1974)

ALL RIGHTS RESERVED
NO PART OF THIS PUBLICATION MAY BE REPRODUCED, STORED IN A RETRIEVAL
SYSTEM, OR TRANSMITTED IN ANY FORM BY ANY MEANS, ELECTRONIC
MECHANICAL, PHOTOCOPYING, RECORDING OR OTHERWISE
WITHOUT PRIOR PERMISSION OF THE COPYRIGHT HOLDER

PRINTED AND BOUND IN GREAT BRITAIN
COPYRIGHT Peter David Thomas 2007

ISBN 0-9516820-3-2
EAN 9780951682036

British Library Cataloguing in Publication Data
A catalogue record for this book is available from the British Library

Concept, design and production
Peter Thomas

Published by
THOMAS CASTLE
5 Abbey Road, Exeter, Devon Ex4 7BG

The Isca Historical Photographic Collection
www.iscacollection.co.uk

Established in 1974 The Isca Collection is the largest private historical photographic archive relating to the City of Exeter. The Collection was originally set up to preserve the work of the Exeter photographer Henry Wykes who operated from the Wykes Studio in Northernhay Place, Exeter recording the city from the turn of the century. On closure of the studio in 1974 the negative stock was estimated at around 42,000 images. Over a thirty year period this has been considerably enlarged and may exceed 60,000 which also include archive and modern images covering Exeter, Devon and Dorset. The Collection contains many of the city's rarest images and covers the city from 1860 to the current time.

The Isca Collection has been the source for many of the city's most noted books on local history as well as the first Videos and DVDs to be produced. Many exhibitions have been staged and lecturing on the Collection and the city's history has continued over the years.

The Isca Collection has been the focus of media attention on many occasions and assistance has been given with documentaries, radio broadcasts, theatrical productions, historical newspaper supplements, written articles and other media activities.

The Collection continues to grow and it is the hoped that an opportunity will arise in the future to set the *Isca Historical Photographic Collection* up as a specific attraction and resource in Exeter for future generations.

ACKNOWLEDGEMENTS

My sincere thanks to

The Express & Echo
Drew Pearce
The Tanning Salon
Ford Simey
Mr D Simms
Mrs L Till

THIS BOOK IS DEDICATED TO NIC

60 YEARS OF PRINCESSHAY

On May 4th 1942 the central area of Exeter was severely bombed. All the remaining standing buildings in the vicinity were removed leaving a vast open derelict space from just above St Stephens Church to the London Inn Square. The cleared area was used for casual car parking for a period, especially around the site that once was Bedford Circus with the enormous, covered Bedford Garage behind. The garage entrance had been in Catherine Street. In upper High Street had stood the Victorian Post Office and the 1881 East Gate Arcade consisting of twenty one shops, with an impressive gateway off High Street. The Arcade backed on to the extensive St Johns School playground also entered from High Street and continued down the length of Southernhay.

Catherine Street joined with Bampfylde Street taking its name from the medieval Bampfylde House, latterly a museum, standing at the junction with Catherine Street.

Anxious to rebuild after the blitz the City Council asked the eminent Town Planner Thomas Sharpe to draw up plans for the regeneration of Exeter. In 1946 a public enquiry discussed the acquisition of land for compulsory purchase and a new Planning Officer, Mr Harold Gayton was employed. A completely new look was to be given to the city centre based on some of Sharpe's plans. A major attraction was to be a pedestrian shopping precinct, one of the first built in the country in the post war period.

In 1949 a special commemorative feature was built off Bedford Street to mark the redevelopment that consisted of a small paved square with a plinth, seating and two dwarf flower beds. A bronze Commemorative plaque was to be fixed to the plinth. When first constructed the feature stood isolated in the open landscape. On the 21st October 1949 HRH Princess Elizabeth Duchess of Edinburgh duly opened the project turning the last screw to fix the plaque and naming the development PRINCESSHAY (Hay being an ancient word for an enclosed open space).

The new shopping precinct took twelve years to construct with the eastern end being the first section to be completed. It consisted of six shops facing into Princesshay. The northwest section, towards Bedford Street, incorporated arcading to protect shoppers from the elements. The south east corner was taken up by Hughes Garage incorporating a multi storey car park. To the rear the new Post Office Street was constructed, with the city wall on the south side. A central archway leading into Southernhay was later widened to allow vehicle access into the new Southernhay Car Park, created on the site of the destroyed Regency Terraces. In 1960 the substantial building East Gate House was opened and the precinct was up and running.

The dominating feature of the new Princesshay was the fine view from east to west down the precinct to the cathedral. It was one of the most impressive views from any shopping centre in the country and had been created due to the foresight of Thomas Sharpe the Town Planner. The precinct was laid out from a datum mark set in the paving of the commemorative feature, with lamp posts placed centrally to line up with the north tower of the cathedral. This could be easily aligned by eye.

A wide variety of shops and offices in Princesshay were to cater for the needs of Exeter residents and visitors for over 40 years and provided a safe and traffic free area.

History was reflected in this prime location with a large statue of Henry V11 attached to the façade of East Gate House marking his relationship with Exeter. It was created for the opening in 1960. The statue is currently lying in the City Council Yard at Belle Isle. Inserted into the pavement below Henry V11 was a brass plaque relating to the royal connection. A further plaque was fixed in the pavement marking the original line of the city wall that was removed after the Second World War. A line of crazy paving crossed the top of Princesshay to the corner Bastion (tower) in Post Office Street.

At East Gate a substantial modern granite plinth stood holding a large Art Deco bronze shield giving the history of East Gate and the Perkin Warbeck Rebellion of 1497. Pre-war the plaque had been fixed to the façade of the Mark Rowe premises that stood on the opposite side of High Street. It is suggested that four plaques were created to mark the site of the city gates for Queen Victoria's Jubilee in 1897.

Fixed to the wall of the entrance to East Gate House was another plaque marking the erection of the building in 1960. At this period the line of the city wall, that had been demolished, was to be marked by a line of crazy paving that extended from High Street to the corner bastion. The remains of the wall hindered the redevelopment and was removed.

Near the top of Princesshay a Blue Boy statue on a plinth was unveiled in October 1957. The name "Blue Boy "was the given to pupils who attended St Johns school in the 17th century and the statue was placed on the site of the former entrance door to the school .The building was destroyed during the Blitz on May 4th 1942.

Fixed to the façade of Hughes Garage in Princesshay, above the entry to the arcade leading to Post Office Street, was a large golden Phoenix with spreading wings, a symbolic bird, marking the rise of the garage from the ashes in 1957 on their pre-war site.

On entering Princesshay from Bedford Street two striking female statues could be seen fixed at first floor level on the north and south façade corners. "Despair" covered her face from the destruction of war whilst opposite, on the south side, "Hope" held a lit beacon reflecting hope for the future.

In Bedford Street two further plaques were found fixed to the Post Office wall on the south end. One stating that a Dominican Convent had stood on the location of the former Bedford Circus and that Princess Henrietta was born on the site. The other plaque, fixed below, related that the plaque above had been fixed to a building in Bedford Circus until it was destroyed by enemy action in 1942.

In the 1980s Exeter's mild climate allowed a new initiative, the planting of cacti in the Princesshay flower beds by the City Council's Parks Dept. The precinct was decorated by floral displays throughout the summer months with flower beds and suspended flower baskets. Exeter was to gain a reputation as a "floral city" but this is now not actively pursued.

In 1991 it was suggested that a Memorial Fountain should be built to commemorate those who lost their lives in the Exeter Blitz and that it should be situated at the top of Princesshay near the site of East Gate. A steering group consisting of the City Council, businesses and The Civic Society raised funds. A horse shoe shaped bronze effect fibre glass fountain designed by sculptor Roger Dean was put in operation on November 19th 1992. Developed with the help of specialist engineers the fountain was controlled from an underground chamber housing pipes and control gear for the water jets. The functioning of the fountain water jets was to prove erratic over a period of time and was eventually switched off.

Exeter's well known Princesshay was razed to the ground in 2006 to make way for a controversial new development and with it went the memories of many Exeter people. This contemporary photo book is not only an "aide memoir" for citizens to reflect on post war rebuilding with limited budgets, and also to recognize and commemorate past events, but will give the opportunity to compare and discuss "old with new" now the redevelopment is complete.

60 YEARS OF PRINCESSHAY continues the work of the Isca Collection to record Exeter and preserve the city's visual heritage.

Peter Thomas
Author
Exeter
2007

Princesshay Construction 1949–1962

Top left: The site of Bedford Circus

Top right: Bedford Chapel

Opposite: High Street cleared of all standing buildings after the Exeter Blitz of May 1942

Left: The central area

Marking the start of rebuilding 1949

Building of the Commemorative feature 1949

Commemorative feature and parked cars 1949

Princess Elizabeth at Exeter 21st October 1949

Opposite: Princess Elizabeth opening Princesshay development 21 October 1949

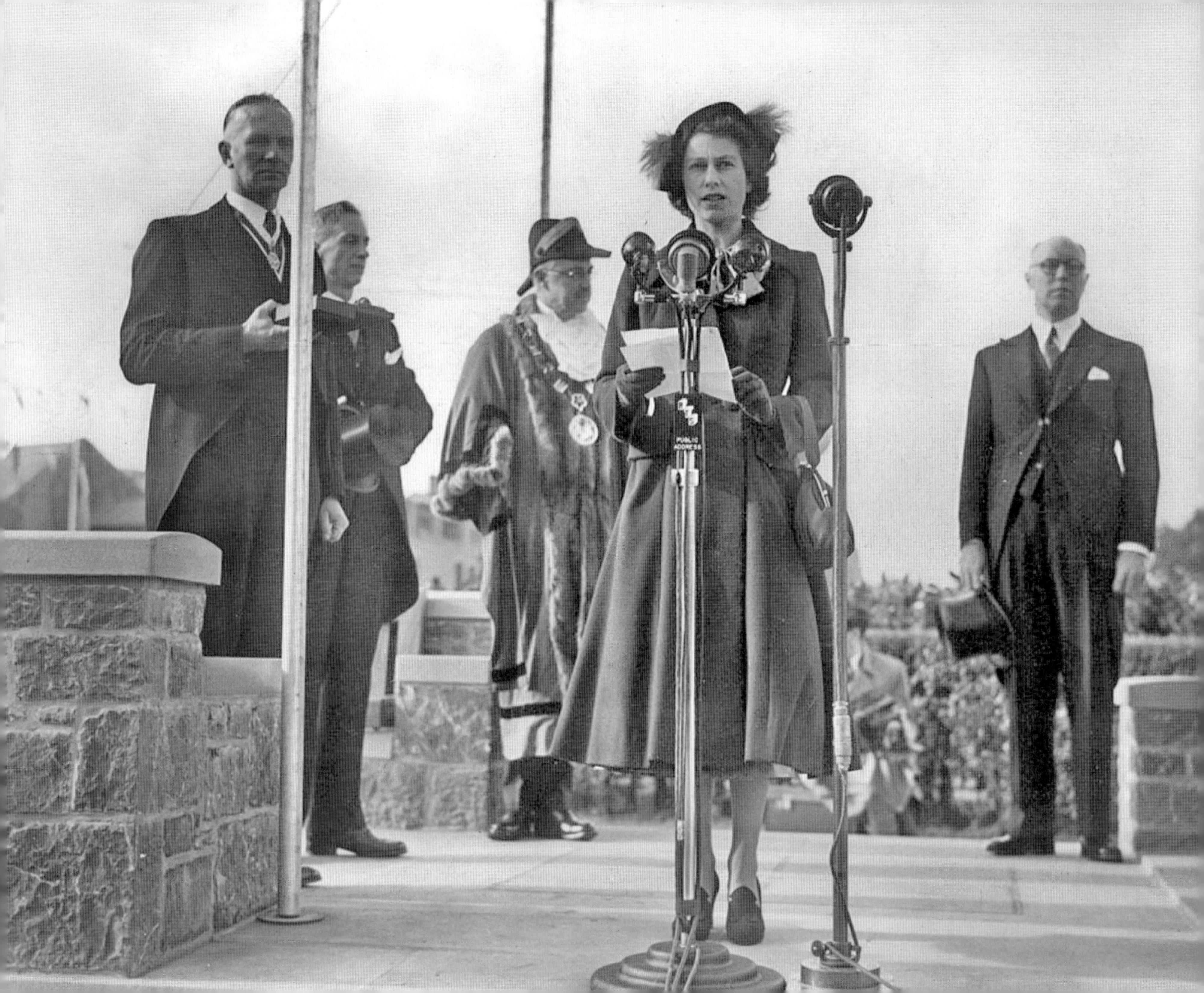
PUBLIC ADDRESS

Sewers being laid on the site for Princesshay

Bedford Street to East Gate

Opposite: View of the Cathedral East to West

9

Completion of North east block

Foundations for Hughes Garage

Opposite: Princesshay south side prior to building of Hughes

Building of Hughes Garage

Post Office Street prior to rebuilding

FRANK WHITE
ARTHUR HUNT
M. MICHAELS
CHANDLERS
H.E. RANDALL Ltd
MAYNE
SAND & GRAVEL

Opposite: Hughes Garage

People watching construction

People on overhead walkway

14

15

Start of building south side shops

Opposite: Princesshay at the junction with the central arcades

SHO
Being Erected on
Please Apply Sole
HALES & PAR
315 7. OXFORD S

Excavation of the city wall

Opposite: View to East Gate

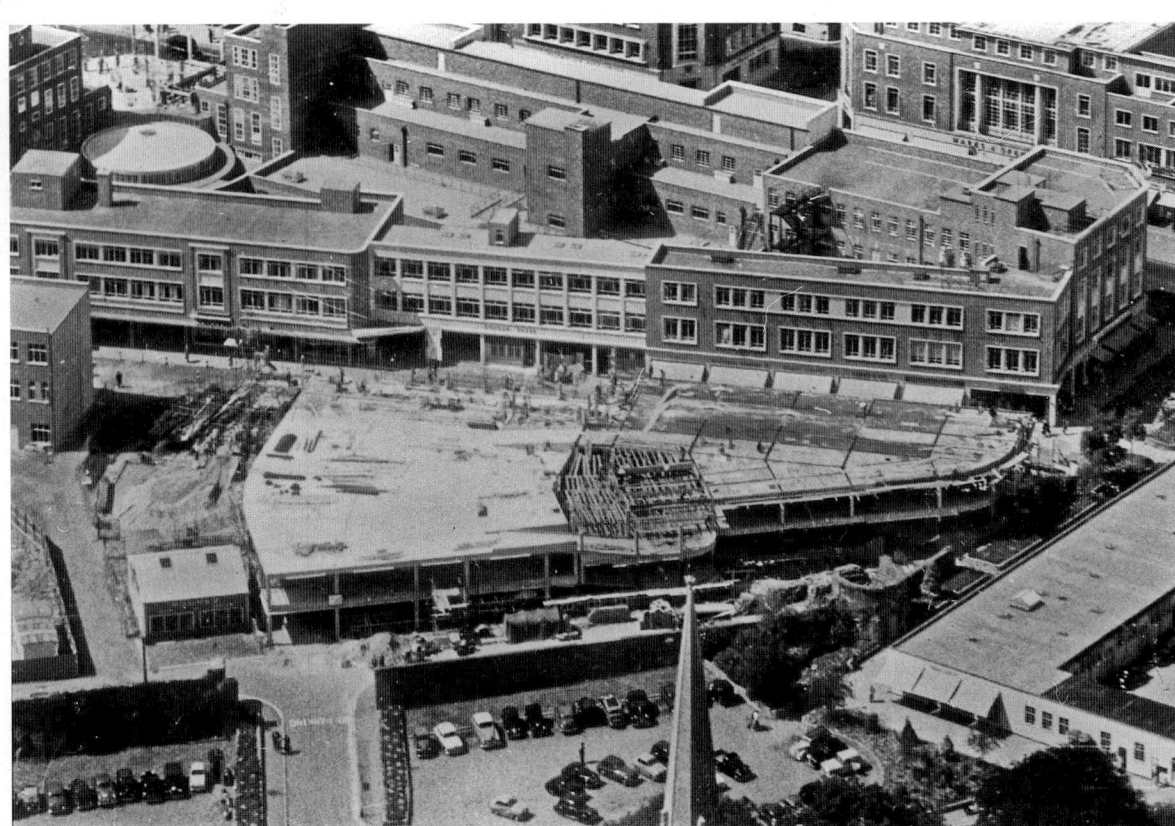

Nearing completion of the multi-storey car park

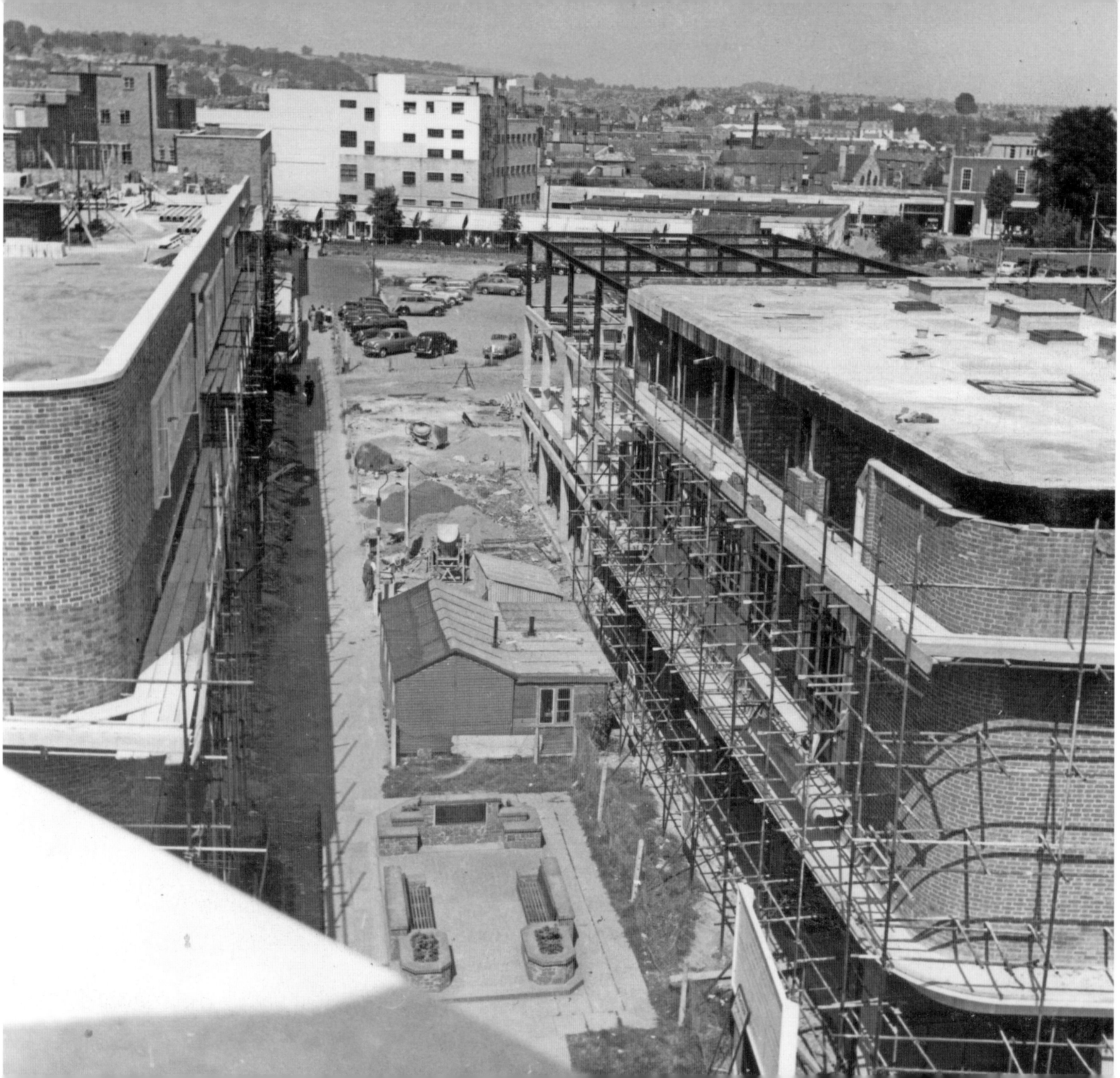

20

Opposite: View from Bedford Street c 1958

Start of paving c 1952

Paving nearing completion

Construction of central seating

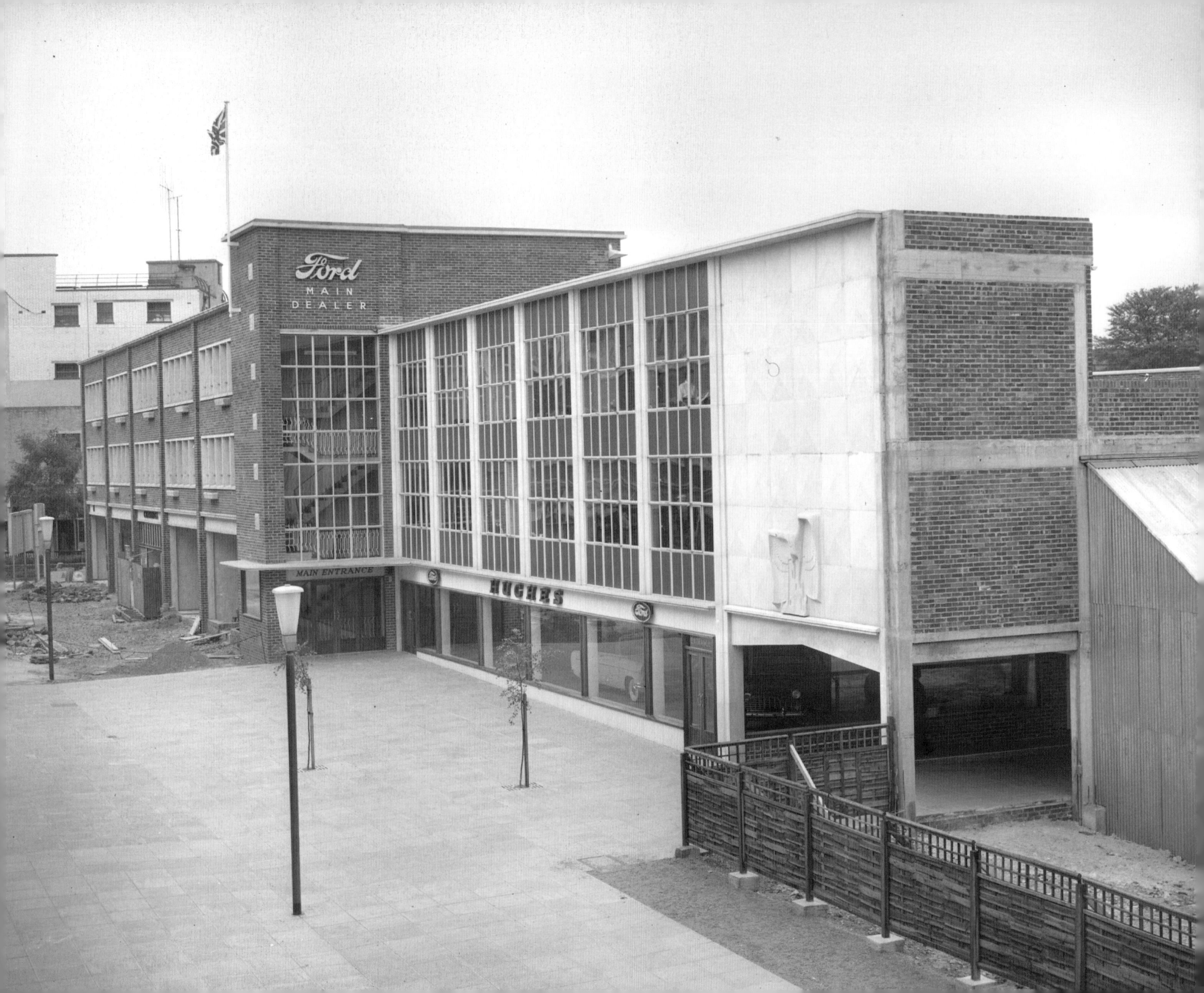

Ford
MAIN
DEALER
MAIN ENTRANCE
HUGHES

Aerial Views of Construction

Early aerial view of the central area

Opposite: Hughes Garage completed

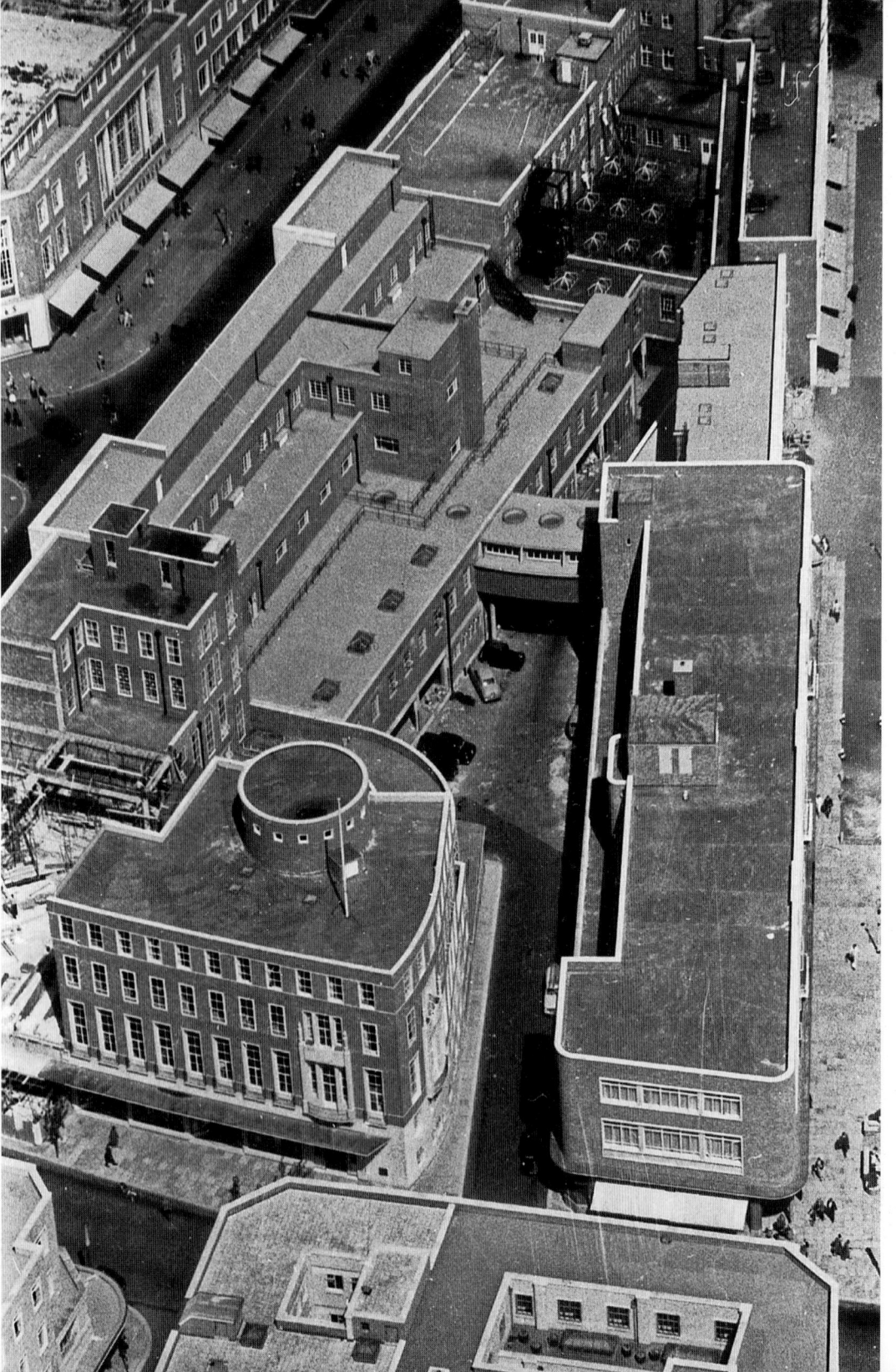

The service road entered from Bedford Street

Opposite: Start of building c 1950

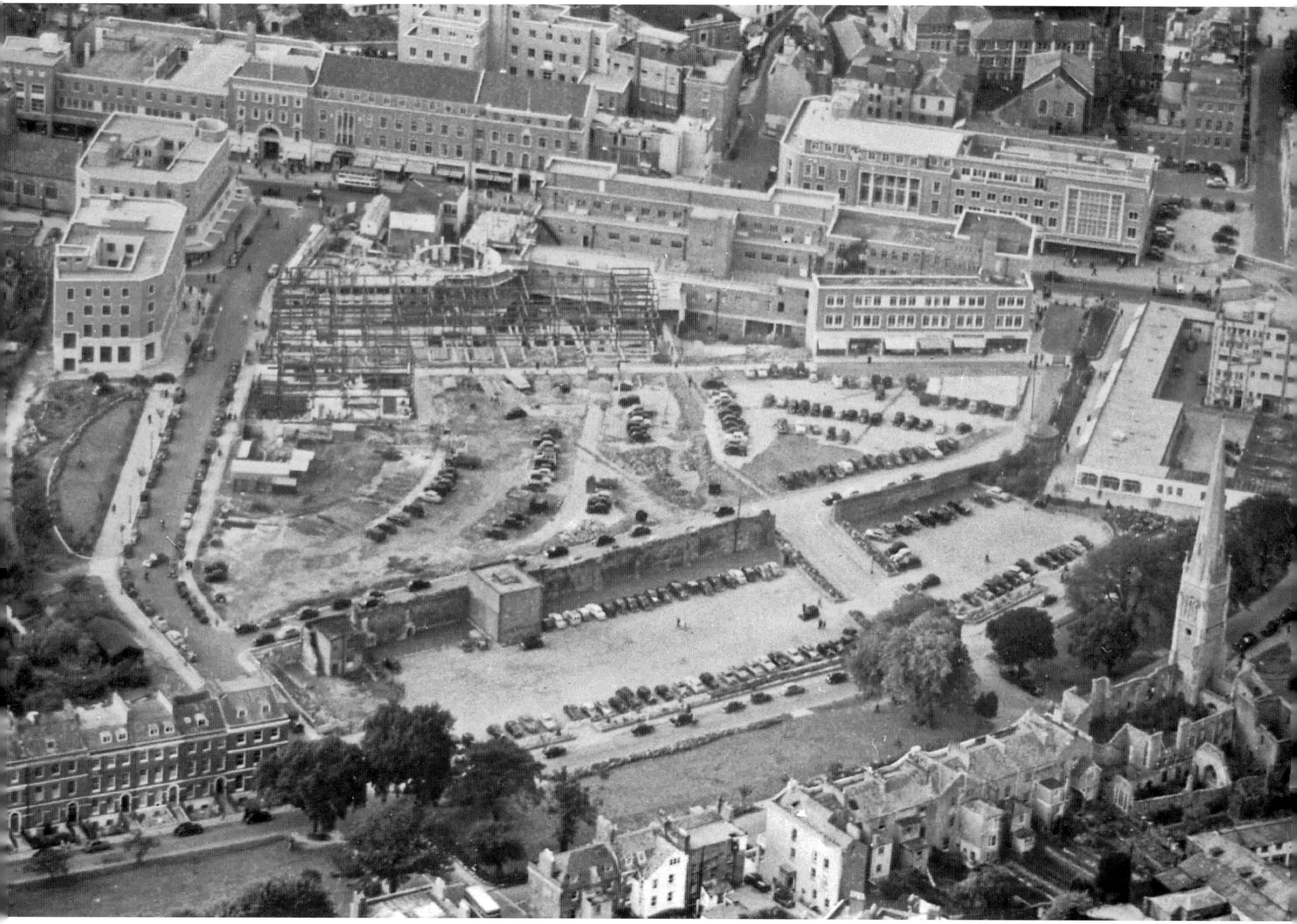

The Post Office site

Temporary shops at Eastgate

Southernhay to Princesshay

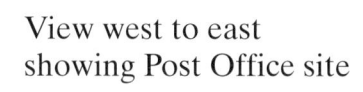

View west to east showing Post Office site

Princesshay development nearing completion

Opposite: Central view

31

Overview Southernhay to Princesshay

Cathedral to Princesshay

High Street and Bedford Street

Princesshay completed

Development of the central area completed c 1962

Princesshay and Area over 60 Years

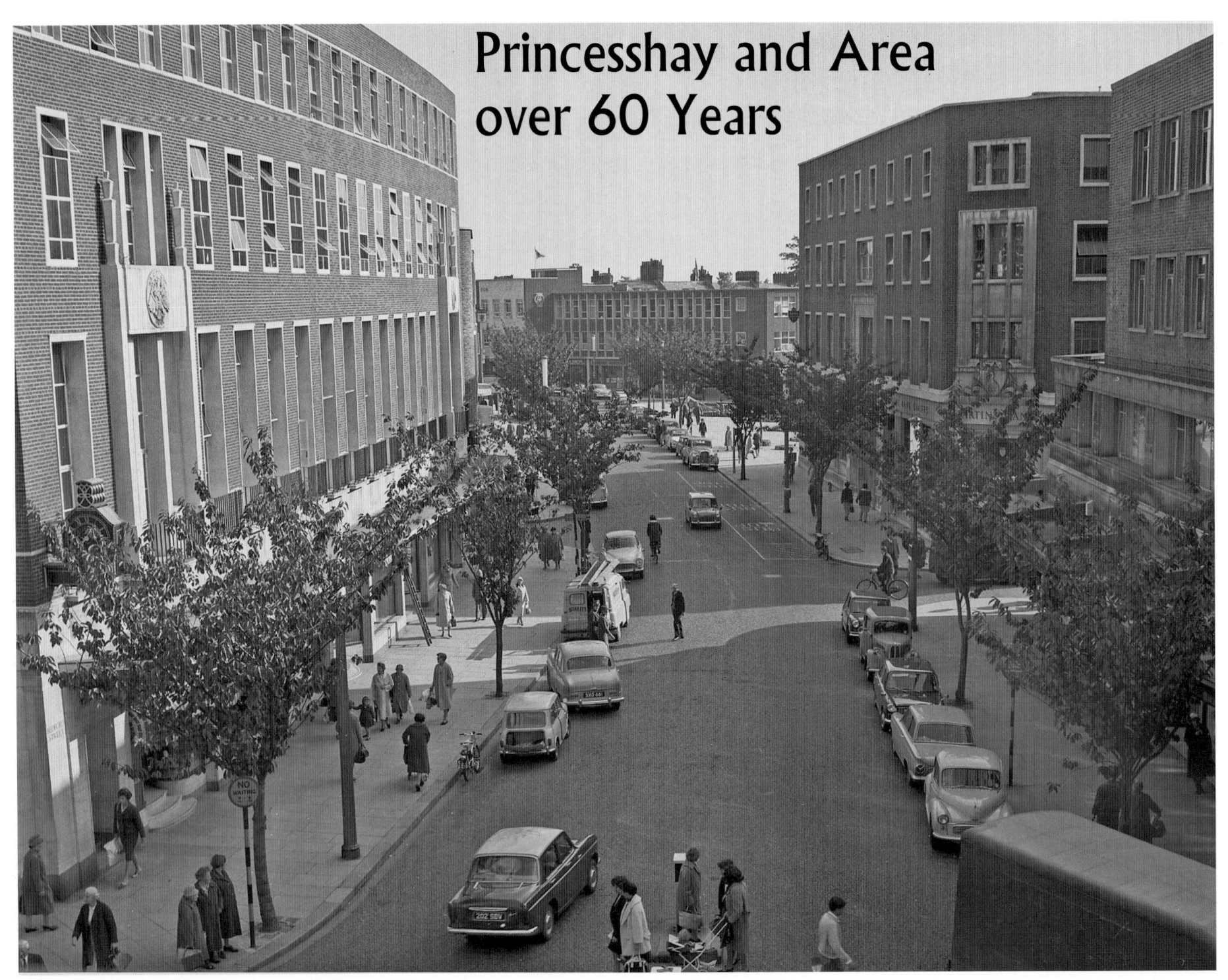

High Street to Bedford Street c 1960

Top left: Bedford Street c 1960

Bottom left: Lamps and flowers at Brufords

Bottom right: High Street to Bedford Street c 1960

Bedford Street and Post Office –1960s

Two plaques on Post Office wall, one stating site of Dominican Convent and birthplace of Princesshay Henrietta. Second plaque related to wartime damage

Bedford Street 2005

Entrance to Post Office

Blue Coat lane from Bedford Street

Opposite: Bedford Street north to south

Royal Coat of Arms at Blue Coat Lane

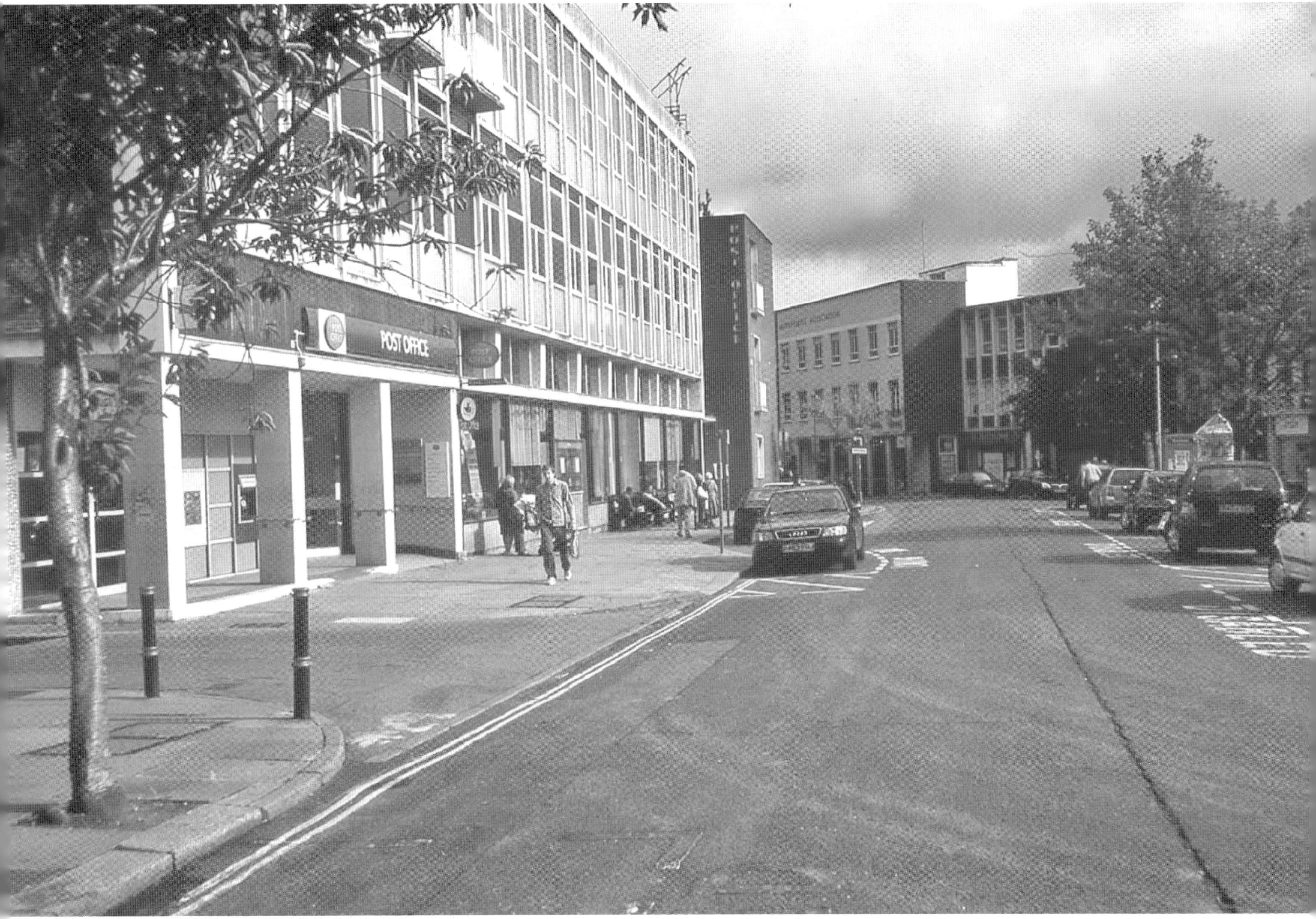
POST OFFICE
POST OFFICE

View across Bedford Street to Cathedral

Bedford Street to Cathedral

Bedford Street west side with sunken piazza

Nos 46–50 Bedford Street

Bedford Street south looking west

City wall and Post Office Street

Sandwich shop at the junction
with Chapel Street

Mosaic by Elaine Goodwin,
Broadwalk House car park

Mosaic by Elaine Goodwin

Top left: Car park Southernhay c 1970

Top right: Post Office Street with city wall and bastion c 1978

Princesshay to Post Office Street

Bedford Street to Cathedral

Bedford Street showing District Bank c 1970

Bedford Street shops 2005

View to Cathedral with District Bank

49

Bedford Street west side

Sunken piazza Bedford Street looking south

Piazza looking south

Entry to Princesshay showing statue of Hope

Statue of Hope

Statue of Hope

Princesshay to Cathedral 1960s

Statue of Despair

ON THE 21st DAY OF OCTOBER 1949
THIS TABLET WAS SET HERE BY
HER ROYAL HIGHNESS
THE PRINCESS ELIZABETH
DUCHESS OF EDINBURGH
TO MARK THE BEGINNING OF THE REBUILDING
OF THE CITY
LARGELY DESTROYED BY ENEMY AIR RAIDS
IN APRIL — MAY 1942

Commemorative plaque

The Phoenix at Hughes Garage

Opposite: Commemorative feature opened 21st October 1949

Above: Entry to underground passages opened 1960

Left: Northcott Theatre Box Office

Line of demolished city wall marked by crazy paving

Eastgate House opened 1960

Statue of Henry VII placed on Eastgate House 1960

Henry VII statue by sculptress Sonja Newton of Dunsford

Plaque at Eastgate House

Electronic signboard at Eastgate facing High Street

Bronze East Gate plague facing High Street

Façade of Eastgate House

EASTGATE HOUSE
1960

ERECTED ON THE SITE
OF THE OLD EAST GATE
EXETER
BY RUISLIP DEVELOPMENT
COMPANY LIMITED
56 GROSVENOR STREET
LONDON W1

ARCHITECTS
DALLING AND PARTNERS
14 BLOOMSBURY SQUARE
LONDON WC1

Opposite: Eastgate House and Princesshay court looking towards Southernhay

Inset: Eastgate House plaque

The Phoenix Fountain turned-on 19th November 1992

Fountain detail

Woman and child at Phoenix Fountain

Children watch water jets

New tourist signposts at Eastgate 1990s

Eastgate and High Street c 1960

Princesshay west to east – mid 1960s

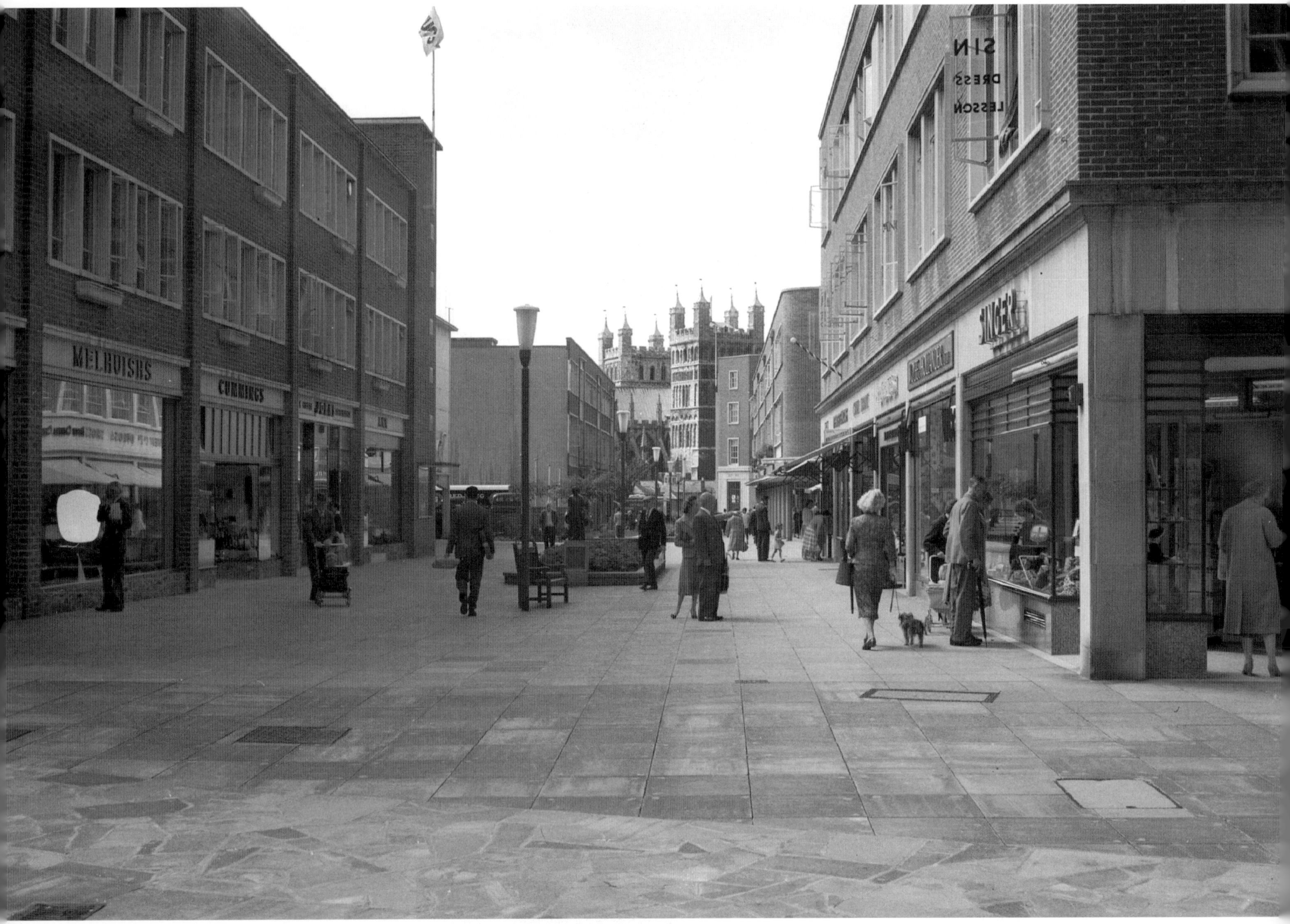
MELHUISHS
CUMMINGS

Flower beds 1970s

Café-style seating 1990s

Opposite:
Princesshay east to west – mid 1970s

Central lampposts Princesshay c 1970

Opposite: View down precinct 1979

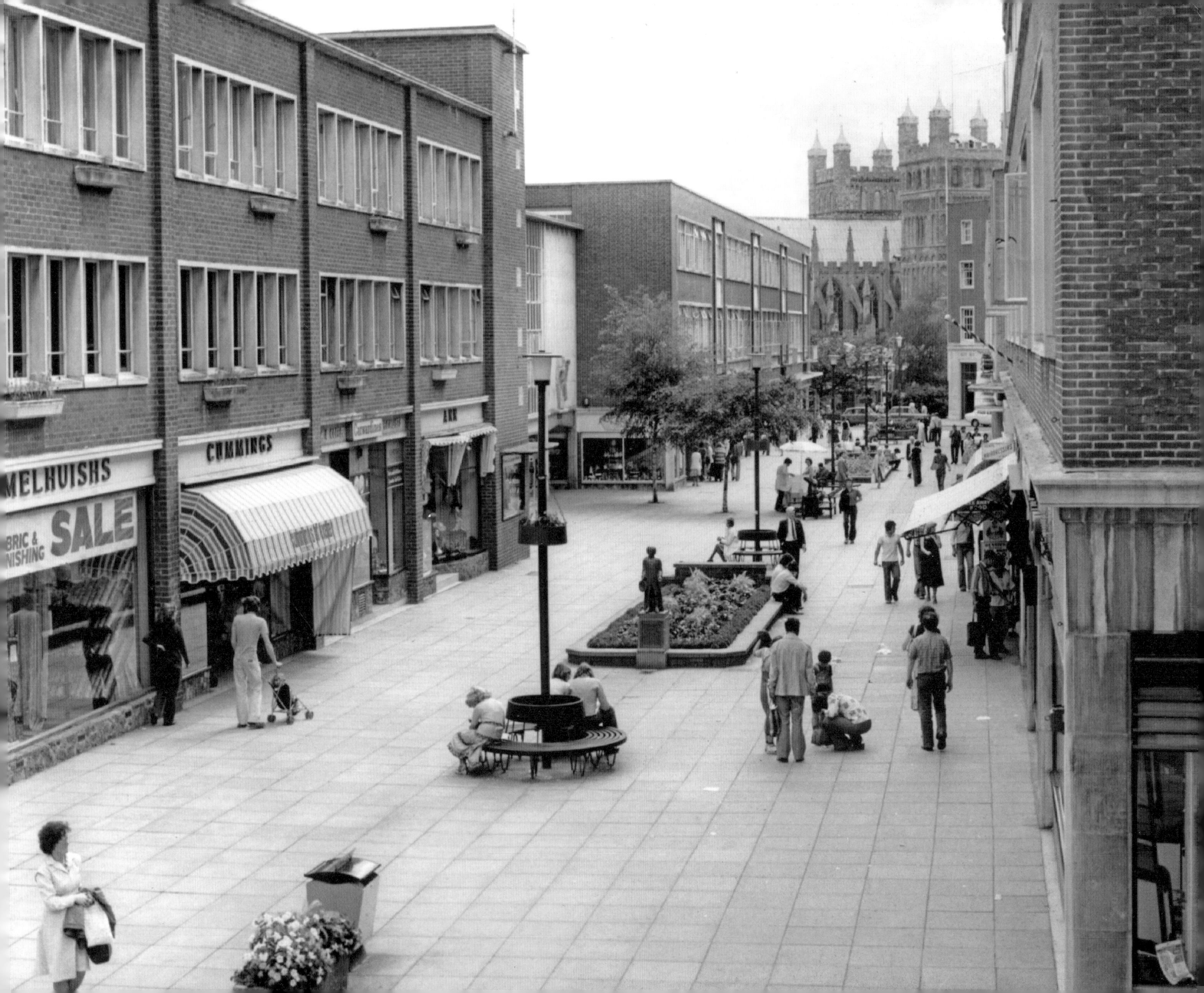
MELHUISHS
SALE
CUMMINGS

Flower bowls

Blue Boy statue marking original site of entrance to St Johns School

Floral Princesshay

Central flower beds

View showing unfinished building work (fenced area)

Outside eating 1995

71

Exeter Festival decorations c 1990

Blue Boy statue

Floral Exeter

Floral Exeter

Relax and enjoy

Floral Exeter

Café society

75

Top left: Flower baskets and beds

Top right: Resting after shopping

Trees and arcading

Early summer

Precinct centre

Strolling

Lampposts and flowers

View of Princesshay from Eastgate House

Cathedral and Princesshay from Eastgate House

Overview of Princesshay

CHRIS HOWES (EXETER)

MAIN DEALERS FOR

ASAHI PENTAX

11 PRINCESSHAY EX1 1NQ

TEL: EXETER 57379

M. MICHAELS
Tel.: 54492

FURS OF RELIABLE QUALITY AT MODERATE PRICES

FINEST SHEEPSKIN, SUEDE AND LEATHER GARMENTS

Repairs and Remodelling by Experts on the Premises. First-class Workmanship

7 PRINCESSHAY · EXETER

Also at TORQUAY. Tel.: Torquay 22207

FOR THE BEST SELECTION OF MACS AND RAINCOATS

come to

THE WEST OF ENGLAND RUBBER CO. LTD

Rainwear Specialists

Agents for: DANNIMAC, QUELRAYN, BARACUTA, WETHERDAIR, ETC.

12-13 QUEEN STREET
EXETER   Phone 73955
(NEXT TO THE CIVIC HALL)

18 PRINCESSHAY
EXETER   Phone 59624

Austin Photographic

AUSTIN PHOTOGRAPHIC.

19 CATHEDRAL YARD, EXETER, EX1 1HB.

PHONE: 55109.

Devon Camera Centre Ltd (The), 29 Prin-

Top left: Eastgate to High Street

Top right: Arcading

Left: Snow in Princesshay

Right: Cacti near Post Office Street junction

82

Aspects of Retail Business in Princesshay

Top left: Arcade leading to High Street

Top middle: Devon Camera Centre

Top right: High Street arcade looking north

Middle left: Arcade looking south

Bottom left: Canns – Eclipse 2000 – Chinese Medical Centre

Bottom right: Local historian, Hazel Harvey, chatting in Princesshay

Left: Bedford House entrance; *Centre:* Pastimes; *Right:* Empty central shops north side

Left: Northcott Theatre Booking Office at East Gate

Centre: The Kitchen

Right: Blue Boy Gift Shop

Far left: Cummings

Left: Chris Howes Photographic

Below: Closure of Princesshay 14/02/05

Middle left: Night time near Christmas

Bottom left: Weigh & Save

85

Demolition of Princesshay and Area 2005–2006

Top left: Bedford Street south

Top right: Demolition at the junction of Chapel Street

Bottom left: Digger in action

Bottom right: Drew Pearce property isolated

Bedford Street from Post Office Street

Top left: Chapel Street after demolition

Top right: Overview of Bedford Street west

Left: View of Post Office from rear of Cathedral Close

Closure of Princesshay 14/02/05

Scaffolding of Princesshay corners

Screening of Princesshay

Opposite: Beginning of demolition

Phoenix Fountain and site store

Closure of High Street Arcade
14/02/05

WRING
GROUP
DEMOLITION

Demolition of lower Princesshay north side

Start of demolition

Removal of buildings north side

Workmen on high platform

Entry to closed Princesshay site

Princesshay as a rubble site

Removal of north side

Time for a chat

Removing Hughes Garage

North east block

Above: Demolition adjoining service road off Bedford Street

Below: Nearing completion

Above right: Cleaning up

Below right: 'Can't believe it is gone'

Opposite: Memories

Damping down

Rubble on the central area

View to Eastgate House

98

99

Site office at
Broadwalk House

Opposite: Bedford Street
to Cathedral

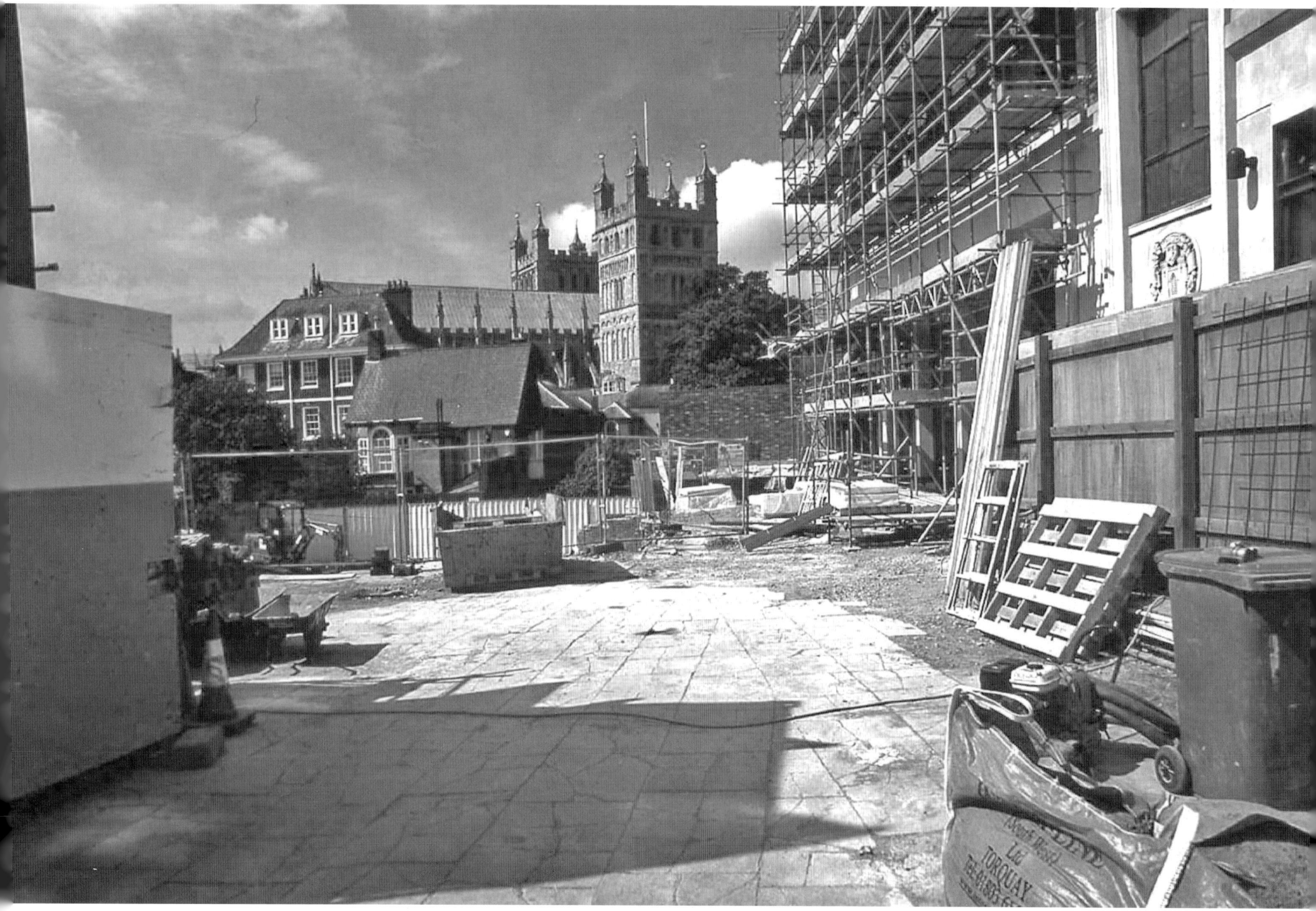
TORQUAY

Above: Chapel Street to Post Office

Above: Post Office shell

Below: Post Office removal

Below: Post Office with archaeologists

Remains of Post Office

Above: Dismantling ancient Exeter

Below: Rubble heap

Archaeologists

Top left: Entry to car park, Post Office Street
Top right: Decimated centre
Bottom left: Post Office Street after demolition
Bottom right: Site clearance

Panoramic central area

Left: Viewing gallery off High Street

Below: Overview of demolished central area from the west

Above: Eastgate House inspection

Right: Removal of Eastgate House

Left: Phoenix Fountain before removal

Princesshay Court standing

Princesshay Court flats demolished

Ruined block

Paris Street offices

Paris Street site

Demolition in progress

Site entrance Princesshay Court

Eastgate site

Next, Paris Street

Next shop front being removed

114

Excavator at Next

Excavator demolishing Next

Demolition spectacle

Power hose damping down at Next

Excavator on site at Paris Street

Overview of High Street/Paris Street corner

Cleared central area

Top left: View to Cathedral; *Top right:* Final stages of clearance

Bottom left: Last stages of site clearance; *Bottom right:* Next rubble

View to Debenhams from the west

New and Used Cars.
As Ford Main Dealers we carry a wide range of both new and used vehicles.

Intensive Service Unit. Most makes of cars are serviced in just one hour. Book in now and drive with confidence.

24-hour Accident and Recovery Service.
Phone: Exeter 72315

Parts and Accessory Shop. We're sure you'll find just what you are looking for in the Accessory Shop on the 1st floor of our Princesshay showroom.

Car Hire from Hughes with a Hertz Rent-A-Car. New Fords and other makes available.

A COMPREHENSIVE SERVICE TO MOTORISTS FROM

HUGHES
OF EXETER LTD.

Ford MAIN DEALER

PRINCESSHAY
EXETER 58433

EXETER and DISTRICT and EAST DEVON
TOWN, COAST and COUNTRY

FOR PROPERTIES OF ALL TYPES

apply to:—

THOMAS SANDERS,
ANDREW REDFERN & CO., F.A.I.

Chartered Auctioneers and Estate Agents

31 PRINCESSHAY, EXETER

Telephone 58374/5

and at EXMOUTH, OTTERY ST MARY, SEATON and SIDMOUTH

67

APPLY TO

HAARER, MOTTS & Co

For details of all
RESIDENTIAL PROPERTY, BUSINESS PREMISES
BUILDING AND REDEVELOPMENT SITES
IN EXETER AND SOUTH DEVON

Auctioneers, Estate Agents, Surveyors & Valuers

33 Princesshay, Exeter

Telephone 56178/9
and at NEWTON ABBOT, TORQUAY and PAIGNTON

NATIONAL FUR COMPANY

ESTABLISHED 1878

This delightful establishment—new to Exeter and part of a famous family business extending over 76 years — specialises in all that is beautiful and in good taste in fur wear. Individuality predominates and ladies will feel just that personal and intimate atmosphere so desirable and so rare in these days of multiple business and mass production.

National Fur Company LTD.

Specialists in Fine Furs since 1878

2 BEDFORD ST · EXETER
(Corner of Bedford St & High St)

TRADES DIRECTORY.　　267

R. H. CUMMINGS LTD.
34 PRINCESSHAY, EXETER

TRAVEL AND FANCY LEATHER GOODS

- HANDBAGS
- WALLETS
- WRITING CASES
- ATTACHE CASES
- TRUNKS
- SUIT CASES
- BRIEF CASES
- WET PACKS

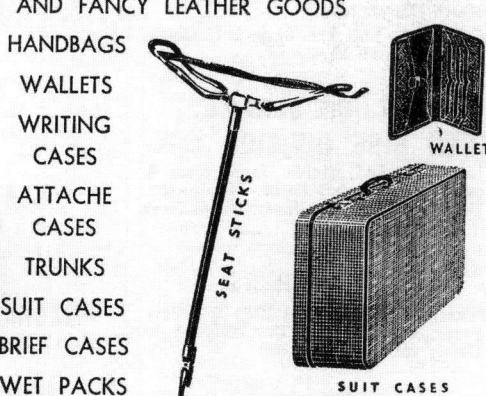

WRITING CASES — WALLETS — SEAT STICKS — BRIEF CASES — SUIT CASES

JEWEL CASES - MANICURE SETS - MUSIC CASES - MASONIC CASES
UMBRELLAS RE-COVERED.　SEAT STICKS, WHIPS, Etc.　ALL REPAIRS

TELEPHONE 73886

open here . . .